DISCOVERING HIGH SCHOOL CROSS COUNTRY

A Comprehensive Guide for the
High School Distance Runner

Kyle M. Rankin, M. Ed.

Discovering High School Cross Country
A Comprehensive Guide for the High School Distance Runner

print ISBN: 979-8-35094-314-6
ebook ISBN: 979-8-35094-315-3

Contents

DISCOVERING HIGH SCHOOL CROSS COUNTRY

A Comprehensive Guide for the High School Distance Runner

My first marathon at the age of 14 – Paul Bunyan Marathon in Bangor, Maine

Dedication

To my dad, Dan Rankin, who was coaching track and cross country before I was even born. I can say with great certainty that my own running career never would have developed as it did had he not taken up running at the same time. He served as my official/unofficial coach throughout my high school years. He has logged nearly 60,000 miles over the past 40+ years and continues to be an avid fan of the sport to this day. Thanks Dad!

Introduction

I began my own running career at the age of twelve. I remember my very first run as if it were yesterday. I jogged a half mile down Atlantic Avenue in Boothbay Harbor, Maine before having to stop to rest for a while. I then turned around and walked and jogged the half mile back home. It was nothing particularly impressive and I don't recall having ever intended for it to be anything more than a one-time activity. But then I did it again the next day, and the day after that. Several months later I won my first ribbon at a local AAU cross-country meet. It was a white ribbon, 4th place. There may well have only been four kids in the race on that particular day but in my mind there were dozens. Regardless, I was hooked. As one who had not experienced a great deal of success at other sports by that age, I'd stumbled onto something good.

Over the coming years, running was everything to me. It taught me the importance of hard work, commitment, and dedication. It taught me how to win and how to lose. It gave me self-confidence while simultaneously teaching me humility. It gave me physical fitness. It taught me how to be a leader and, when appropriate, a follower. It gave me lifelong friendships with countless teammates and coaches. It changed my life.

I was very fortunate in that my Dad discovered running at about the same time that I did. He and I travelled countless miles to run in various road races throughout my early teens. Those are memories that I would never give back.

I benefitted tremendously from being part of what was a very strong running community in Maine at that time. For a state with a population that hovers around only a million, Maine has some of the most talented and toughest runners that I've ever seen, even to this day. Think along the lines of Joan Benoit Samuelson, Andy Palmer, and Bruce Bickford.

Before injuries eventually forced me from the competitive side of our sport, I'd run nearly 50,000 miles. I'd run in more than 400 races ranging in distance from the mile to the marathon. I'd competed all across the country, running against many of the best runners of the time.

If there is an injury to be had, I probably had it. If there is a race to be run, I probably ran it. I've experienced those thrilling championships and record-breaking performances. I've suffered through those agonizing defeats and inevitable heartbreaks that our sport brings with it. I have done so both as a runner and now, more recently, as a coach.

With my own competitive days long since behind me, my aim now is to give something back to the sport that has given me so much. "Pay it forward," as they say. If, in ten or twenty years, even just one of the student-athletes that I have worked with is able to look back upon his or her own days as a high school runner as fondly as I do my own, I will have truly won.

Even during my earliest days as a runner, I had a keen sense of understanding as to how important "experience" is in this sport of ours.

I have always believed that perhaps in no other sport is experience as valuable an asset as it is in that of distance running.

Of course, "experience," by its very definition, is something that one has to gain on their own. I am hopeful, however, that my own experience, both as a runner and as a coach, can be helpful to today's young runners, perhaps by helping to flatten out the learning curve or by preventing them from making some of the same simple mistakes that I may have made along the way.

It is not my intention to delve too deeply into, nor belabor, any single topic within the limitations of this writing. I will leave much of the intricate, detailed science of our sport to those who are more qualified to address those issues. In several cases, I have knowingly glazed over a given topic rather than risking getting stuck in the weeds. View this writing as an introduction to a wide variety of running-related concepts with more details to follow.

Many of the "chapters" may hardly be chapters at all, merely a few short paragraphs. Though I will address training patterns and concepts in a broad-ranging sense, I don't plan to include many detailed day-by-day training plans. Those are perhaps best saved for subsequent editions. You'll find that the same is true as I discuss various concepts related to competition and team structure.

My aim is to address high school cross country specifically, and distance running more generally, from an angle that perhaps others have not. I am hopeful that the following pages are both informative and inspirational for coach and student-athlete alike. My intention is to address neither the elite high school athlete nor the beginner specifically. The theories and concepts that I present herein are intended to apply to all equally.

There may well be coaches and young runners who have achieved great success by approaching our sport from a completely different angle. Perhaps there will be those who take issue with some aspect of my approach to our sport. I wish those coaches and young runners nothing but the best and I congratulate them on their success. That's one of the great things about our sport. There is no one single right way of doing things. The conversation is always open. What works best for one does not necessarily mean that it is what is going to yield the best results for others.

Enjoy the experience, both as a coach and as a young runner. As I was lucky enough to have done some 45 years ago, you have stumbled onto something good.

Coach Rankin and Chase Howes talking it over after a meet. A sophomore at the time, Chase would later break his high school's 1,600-meter record as a senior.

CHAPTER ONE

Distance Running is Not a Seasonal Activity

For many years I have found myself telling my student-athletes and their parents, "If I were ever to write a book about distance running and, more specifically, about high school cross country, Chapter One would focus solely on the concept that "Distance Running is Not a Seasonal Activity," at least not for those who aspire to reach their fullest potential as runners. Well, here we are, Chapter One.

Over the years, specialization within the youth sports environment has, in many cases, reached the point of absurdity. Does that six-year-old kid really need to be playing soccer year-round? Does he or she need to be on a summer travel team, simultaneously playing on club teams while competing as part of his or her school's team? Probably not. Here, however, I need to be careful for fear of coming across as being a hypocrite. The need for a distance runner who aspires to greatness to continue running year-round is absolute. To be clear, volume and intensity levels may vary considerably season-to-season and there will surely be times of relative rest. Moreover, what he or she is running in February may look nothing like what he or she is running in July. His or her daily training in August will likely differ considerably from what he or she is doing in December. If it doesn't, something isn't quite right. Extended periods of non-running, however, are best avoided at most any cost. We will talk about these concepts in more detail later as we address periodization.

I love baseball. I played baseball as a kid prior to discovering running. In the interest of making my point, let's assume that I am playing baseball at the high school level and my season ends today. If I so choose, I can put my equipment away for several weeks, maybe even a couple of months, not picking up a glove, ball or bat for an extended period of time. Eight to ten weeks from now, maybe I decide that it's time to start getting back into baseball shape again. If you give me ten days in the batting cages, I will likely have begun to catch up to the fastball again and my arm will rapidly be gaining strength on a path to where it was when my season ended nearly three months ago. Distance running doesn't work that way. Yes, there are absolutely times of the year when some relative rest and recovery, both mental and physical, is what is appropriate. It is when those couple of weeks of relative downtime turn into months and/or "relative downtime" becomes "absolute downtime" that we are really doing ourselves a disservice as distance runners. Not only is it going to take us an extended period of time to get back to where we were previously from a conditioning standpoint, but we are going to find that we are suddenly much more prone to nagging injuries, the types of injuries that are more commonly associated with those who are just getting started in our sport. We are likely to be frustrated, discouraged, and out of shape.

To be clear, I am not suggesting that everyone on a given high school cross country team needs to be a fanatical, dedicated, year-round runner aspiring to run at a championship level. Not at all. The opportunity exists for student-athletes of widely ranging athletic abilities to contribute to a cross country program. This year-around notion applies only to those who aspire to realize their highest potential as distance runners. The majority of you who've chosen to begin reading this book fit into that category.

On one occasion while coaching at the high school level, I appointed a young lady who in no way aspired to be a top-notch distance runner to be our girls' team captain. Tiffany was a highly skilled lacrosse player in the spring and viewed cross country merely as a means by which to get into shape during the fall. She alternated between running varsity and JV from week to week and was perfectly comfortable doing so. Her leadership skills and work ethic were such that she was not only a valuable member of our program but also a very well-suited captain.

It should be noted that there is no amount of playing soccer, playing basketball, riding a bike, playing volleyball, or hiking that is going to benefit a runner as much as is actual running. All of those are enjoyable, social, and healthy activities. All burn calories and all will help you keep in shape. None of them, however, regardless of volume, equates to actual running.

The bottom line is this . . . If you take nothing else away from this reading, please make sure that it is a very clear understanding that, for those looking to maximize their potential as distance runners, "Distance Running is Not a Seasonal Activity."

By the end of her junior year in high school, Rilee Morrison had won multiple Conference, District, and Regional championships and was a five-time FHSAA State Championship qualifier.

CHAPTER TWO

Proper Pacing

This could have just as easily been Chapter One. Perhaps in an updated, expanded 2nd edition, it might be. I could likely write an entire book on this subject alone. It's that important. Frankly, this topic is so broad ranging and so important that I am struggling as to exactly where to start.

I learned proper pacing at a very young age, early in my running career, and it helped me tremendously over the years that followed. My dad was a student of the sport and my unofficial coach during my early years as a runner. He very much instilled in me how incredibly important proper pacing can be. Additionally, I was surrounded by a wide variety of knowledgeable, enthusiastic, and highly trained adult runners whom I looked up to and tried to emulate, and of whom I constantly asked questions. The concept of proper pacing seems so basic. Clearly it is not, however. So many young runners have a hard time mastering this ever-so-important concept and they tend to struggle as result. Similarly, there are plenty of coaches who fail to fully appreciate and understand how incredibly important proper pacing can be. It takes an awareness of one's own abilities, it takes self-discipline, and it takes patience and self-confidence. It takes an understanding and appreciation of human body function and it requires a willingness to sometimes sit back and allow others to make pacing mistakes, even if it means that you find yourself well behind your similarly-talented competition early in races. I get it. That's not easy.

Most commonly, when I talk to my student-athletes about proper pacing, I do so in the context of competitive situations. This concept is far more wide-reaching and all-encompassing than that, however. It also applies to your workouts as well as to your daily distance runs.

Let's begin here . . . If I am to drive from Miami to Jacksonville, a distance of some 350 miles, there is a certain speed at which my car will achieve maximum gas mileage and incur a minimal amount of wear and tear. A trained mechanic might suggest that this sweet spot is somewhere in the 55–60 miles-per-hour range, though it is going to depend considerably upon the car. I could set out from Miami at 90 miles per hour. It's going to look like I am making great time but I am also burning fuel at an extremely elevated rate. It's likely that I run out of gas well before I ever reach Jacksonville. My impressive start has turned out to be nothing more than that. Conversely, I could leave Miami at 30 miles per hour and allow my speed to vary wildly over the next several hours: 30 mph, 60 mph, 90 mph. Perhaps I still average 60 miles per hour, but I've done it the hard way. My car hates that constant acceleration and deceleration and it is going to burn more fuel as a result of that kind of driving pattern. Perhaps I still make it to Jacksonville but my car is likely overheated and very low on gas.

As a runner, think of yourself along these same lines. Your body is likely to perform at its best at a constant, steady pace. Not convinced? Ever gone out on a relatively short fartlek run, varying paces, fast-slow-fast, throughout your run only to get back home and find yourself completely wiped out? You didn't go any farther than usual and at no time were you pushing yourself to the point of exhaustion but wow, you're tired. Your body hates that inconsistency, speeding up and slowing down. (It is for this reason that an occasional fartlek run isn't a bad idea as part of a well-rounded training program. You are training the body to perform more efficiently in a manner and in a context in which it is not comfortable).

We have all seen that young runner who feels the need to build a 50-meter lead during the early stages of a cross country meet only to then fade to the middle of the pack by the time he or she has reached the middle of the race. More often than not, he or she ends up finishing well back in the pack, having run much slower than might have been anticipated. That type of thing is likely to happen to a young runner once or twice and that's fine. It's a normal part of the learning process. It is that "experience" that I spoke of earlier.

What I find confusing is when that same runner makes that same mistake again and again and again. Clearly, he or she is not learning and/or trying to make adjustments based upon his or her struggles of earlier meets. Is it simply a lack of understanding? Is it ego? Is it self-discipline? Is it coaching? Is it related to anxiety and nervousness? On one hand, I admire the persistence and the competitive spirit that this runner clearly has but, at the same time, he or she would likely run so much faster were they able to approach the race a little differently.

Here is a side thought . . . have a race plan! Don't necessarily base your own race plan upon what others are doing but have an idea as to where you want to be from a pacing perspective. Do you want to be 6:00 at the first mile or 6:20? "I want to be within 5 seconds of Julia at the mile marker" isn't perhaps the best strategy. What happens if Julia is having a rough day and is nowhere close to you at the mile marker? Or perhaps the opposite is true and she is on her way to a 30-second personal record? To what degree is your initial race plan still viable? Now what do you do? Instead, consider the weather, the level of competition, the condition of the course, and where you are in terms of your own conditioning. Base your own race plan off of those more-dependable variables. I am amazed at how frequently young runners compete without having developed a game plan for that particular meet. It doesn't have to be terribly complex nor scientifically-based but at least have a basic plan in place.

If we were somehow magically able to determine that you are capable of running exactly six-minute pace for the duration of a given 5K (18:36) but you then come through that first mile in 5:35, I am likely going to have some questions for you. Questions like "What are you doing?" Yes, you are now 25 seconds ahead of schedule but you're almost assuredly going to pay a big price for that aggressive start. Your next mile probably fades to 6:25 and your final mile may now be 7:10 or 7:20. Remember, in this scenario we've somehow determined with 100% accuracy that you are capable of running 18:36 on that particular day, assuming that you pace it properly and evenly. As it stands, you will likely now still manage to break 20:00 but it will be close. Not only that, but it will hurt a lot more than it would have had you done a little better job of pacing yourself.

Now, here is the thing about cross country ... unlike running on a track where every lap is just like the one before it in terms of topography, cross country is inherently varying and changing. Hills, mud, turns, deep grass. Perhaps that first mile includes a long downhill? Perhaps there are questions as to how accurately that first mile was measured when the course was laid out? If so, maybe, just maybe, that 5:35 first mile isn't as crazy as it sounds. Those types of things have to be considered. When I talk about proper pacing as it applies to cross country, I always begin the conversation with "All things being equal ..." In cross country, they rarely are.

Please understand, as I do, that there are certain situations that might call for a less-than-conventional race strategy. As an example ... let's suppose that I am competing in a late-season cross country 5K in which I know fully well that several of my fellow competitors have better closing leg speed than I do. Let's say that this is a district championship meet and I have a legitimate shot at qualifying for regionals the next weekend. In order to do so, I know that I am going to need to beat a few of those speedsters. If I follow my usual, evenly-paced race strategy and allow that 5K to become a 400-meter race to the finish, I am almost assuredly going to be outkicked. In this scenario, I am likely going to have to take some risks. Perhaps I go out a bit harder than I might otherwise normally do. Maybe I include a few mid-race surges in the interest of trying to deaden the legs of my fellow competitors, thus reducing their ability to kick at the end. Might I be able to build a significant enough lead so as not to be outsprinted at the finish line? I have to take some chances, chances that I might not otherwise take. Sure, my approach might backfire but desperate times call for desperate measures in this situation.

Going out too hard? Why does it matter? Earlier I promised that this writing would not devolve into a scientific study of human motor behavior nor a convoluted mix of scientific data and terminologies. Here is where I need to be careful that I avoid doing so. When our muscles fire, they produce waste just as our cars produce exhaust when their combustion engines operate. It's happening right now as you sit there reading this chapter. The more aggressive our movements and actions, the more waste our muscles produce. This waste is collectively referred to as "lactate." Our bodies are constantly working to rid themselves of this lactate, primarily through the respiratory process. No matter what kind of physical shape you may be in as a runner, there comes a point during vigorous exercise that your body is now producing lactate more quickly than it can get rid of it. At that point, we have crossed our "lactate threshold." As this happens, maximal performance is going to become more and more difficult to maintain and we will almost assuredly begin to slow down. It is going to take our body a little time to get back to equilibrium, the point at which it has removed enough lactate for our muscles to once again operate at its maximal efficiency. The problem is, specific to track and cross country, we don't have that time. We can't call a timeout at the 800-meter mark of a race. By going out too aggressively at the outset of any given race, we run the risk of having to call a "timeout." We run the risk of falling from 1st place to 10th place to 20th place over the course of the next 2+ miles. Sure, we want to have an empty tank by the time we cross the finish line. We just don't want to be out of gas by the halfway marker.

Look, I get it. You're nervous. You're excited. It's easy to get caught up in the moment. As they line up on the starting line, my last words of advice to my runners is almost always something along the lines of "Run smart. Think about what you're doing."

If you are going to make a "mistake" from a pacing perspective, I'd much prefer that it be an issue of perhaps going out too slowly rather than going out too fast. If you go out too slowly, you still have another 2+ miles to make it up. If you go out too hard, there is relatively little that you can do to effectively change the situation and you may be in for a long, disappointing, painful afternoon. Remember, they don't give awards to those who are leading at the one-mile marker.

Very rarely do the kids that I coach ever hear me talking about my own days as a runner, races that I won, or specific times that I ran. When they do hear me talking along those lines, it is almost always in the interest of trying to make a broader point. The stories that I share are never "Yay for Coach Rankin." Here, in fact, is a quick, topic-appropriate, story that is the exact opposite. . . .

I'd had a pretty good track season during my senior year in high school. I'd gone undefeated in the 1600 within our district, having run a PR (Personal Record) of 4:24 in late April. I was the top seed going into our district meet, holding a healthy seven-second advantage over the number-two-seeded runner. There were several other kids who had run 4:31, 4:32, and 4:33 during the course of the season. As we lined up for the 1600 at the district meet that morning, not only was I the top seed, I was by far the most experienced runner in the field of 16. Two hundred meters into the race I was in 4th or 5th place, perhaps a bit boxed in, but comfortable. We came through 200 in a relatively pedestrian 34 seconds. For whatever reason, I decided to break out of the pack and take the lead. I surged around the far curve and down the near straightaway, coming through the 400 in 61.5 . . . 61.5! That's great if you are looking to run 4:06. I surely wasn't. By 1200 meters I was in trouble, clearly paying the price for my own impatience and relative stupidity of some 800 meters earlier. One of my own team-mates as well as a rival from Episcopal Academy had both passed me. I did what I could to maintain contact but I was running out of time. I knew that I had two things working in my favor, however. While both of the runners ahead of me had significant leg speed, I knew that I was stronger than either of them. Additionally, my ridiculous first lap had also caused both of them to go out too hard. With 200 meters left, I managed to pass the kid from Episcopal and pull up onto my teammate's shoulder. Mark and I sprinted side-by-side for that last 200 meters. Ultimately he beat me by a fraction of a second as we both ran 4:29. The number one seed, the most experienced runner in the race, I'd gotten exactly what I deserved as a result of my own lack of self-control. I knew better. All these years later, I still remember the painful lesson that I learned that day. Perhaps you too can take something away from my blunder of so long ago?

Those are the risks of going out too fast. On the other end of the spectrum, and far less concerning to me quite frankly, is what I've oftentimes heard being referred to as a "freshman finish." It's that kid who is likely new to running and is on his or her way to running a 32:00 5K. Then, suddenly, they run that last 200 meters in near-world-record time, drawing "oohs" and "aahs" from the crowd. That's just a lack of experience. Moving forward, I might challenge him or her to exert a bit more energy earlier in the race, assuring them that doing so might quickly yield a significantly faster time. To be clear, if you've got the energy to kick over that last 200 - 300 - 400 meters, use it, but you want to avoiding having quite that much left at the finish.

Just as proper pacing is a vital part of our race-day strategy, so too does it apply to our everyday training. Suppose we are on the track running 10 x 400 with a 3 minute recovery between each. Those who lack the experience or self-discipline might run that first 400 in 73 or 74 seconds. By the fourth 400 they are now running 84 or 85 seconds. By number 7 they have now fallen off to 90 seconds. It's realistic to anticipate that they might not even make it through the remainder of the workout. That's a tough way to live. Not only is the "pain meter" going to be off the charts but they have failed to complete the workout at all, likely reaping much less benefit as a result. Logic and experience would suggest that they would perhaps be better off starting with an 80 second 400. Number seven is now more likely to be 82 or 83 rather than 90 and the odds of them being able to complete the entire workout increases exponentially.

Your easy distance days are no different. If you've recently managed to run a 20:00 5K PR (6:28 pace), it would make little sense for your daily training runs to be at 7:00 pace. Tempo runs? Maybe. You're probably better off going out for your 5 or 6 miles at a 7:45 - 8:00 pace. Pace yourself appropriately, knowing that what is an ideal pace for one is oftentimes less-than-ideal for another. Am I belaboring this pacing issue a bit? Maybe, but it is that important.

The kids that I have coached over the years have oftentimes heard me refer to "variance" as it relates to their cross country meet performances. I will sometimes even refer to "variance 1" and "variance 2." Some of us, myself included, are numbers people and benefit from having clearly defined data with which to work. This "variance" concept provides exactly that. In reviewing a given student-athlete's meet performance, we will commonly talk in terms of "variance 1," the degree to which, represented in terms of a percentage, their first mile pace varied from their average pace over the entirety of the 5K. "Variance 2," more specifically, represents the degree to which their first-mile time and second-mile time varied. The higher the number, the greater the degree to which they slowed. Reflecting back to what I spoke about earlier and our goal to run a fairly steady, even pace over the course of five kilometers, I encourage a variance of no more than 3 - 4% in most cases. Remember what I said, however, about "all things being equal." In cross country they never are. A more varied, challenging course will almost always yield higher variances. Regardless, those numbers can still be used as valuable points of comparison, one runner to the next.

	Mile 1	Mile 2	(2nd Mile)	Finish	Avg.	Variance
Thomas	5:26	11:05	5:39	17:29	5:39	4.0
Chase	5:35	11:30	5:55	18:15	5:53	5.4
Taylor	5:56	12:15	6:19	18:54	6:06	2.8
Lucas	6:03	12:22	6:19	18:57	6:07	1.1
Gibson	6:24	14:02	7:38	22:59	7:25	15.9
Colin	6:24	12:50	6:26	19:53	6:26	0.5
Charlie	6:36	13:10	6:34	20:12	6:31	1.3
Alex	6:26	13:00	6:34	19:59	6:27	0.2
Landon	6:29	13:24	6:55	20:31	6:37	2.1
Griffin	6:24	13:26	7:02	21:22	6:54	7.8
Christian	8:13	18:42	10:29	30.26	9:51	19.9
Cameron	7:59	19:00	11:01	30.49	9:56	24.4
Leo	6:52	14:48	7:56	23.37	7:37	10.9
Rilee	6:34	13:39	7:05	20:54	6:45	2.8
Ada	7:03	14:30	7:27	22:08	7:08	1.2
Annie	7:03	14:33	7:30	22:37	7:18	3.5
Anisa	7:48	16:36	8:48	25.21	8:10	4.7
Lauren	7:28	15:28	8:00	23:40	7:38	2.1
Addie	7:46	16:06	8:20	24.39	7:57	2.4
Lucciana	8:15	16:42	8:27	25.07	8:06	1.8
Emily	7:37	15:50	8:13	24.21	7:51	3.1
Fifi	8:06	16:30	8:24	25.17	8:09	0.6
Julia	7:57	16:36	8:39	25.25	8:13	3.4
Montana	9:15	20:07	10:52	31.47	10:15	10.8
Anya	8:06	17:05	8:59	26.53	8:40	7.0
Haley	8:12	16:45	8:32	25.28	8:13	2.0
Lily	8:10	17:35	9:25	27.06	8:46	7.3
Brensley	8:45	19:18	10:33	30.53	9:58	13.9
Karen	8:32	20:42	12:10	32.56	10:37	24.4
Riley	9:15	19:34	10:19	30.42	9:54	7.0
Tati	7:48	16:49	9:01	26.35	8:36	10.2

Personal Record
Variance: Represented in terms of seconds. The difference between your first mile and your average mile.
Especially tight Variance

Before moving on to other topics, I want to share a quick story, in part because I find it so entertaining, and in part because it exemplifies the exact and complete polar opposite of "proper pacing."

Gatlinburg, Tennessee used to host a very competitive 10K road race every summer, "Run for the Hills." They gave away a considerable amount of prize money to the top finishers and drew runners from all over the southeast and beyond. It wasn't at all uncommon for elite runners from as far away as Kenya and Ireland to show up at this race. During the summer following our sophomore year at the University of Tennessee, one of my roommates, a guy named Bruce, decided that he wanted to go run in the "Run for the Hills." I opted out but agreed to go watch him run.

Earlier I stated that "they don't give awards to those who are leading at the mile marker." Well, in this case, they did. In the interest of keeping the race as fast and as competitive as possible, they offered a $250 cash prize to whomever was leading the race at the 1 mile marker but . . . that person had to finish the race within the top 20 places in order to receive that payout.

As a runner, Bruce had plenty of leg speed and considerable range but he would be the first to tell you that he was primarily an 800/1500 meter guy. His plan on race day was to be leading at the mile marker, hoping to then be able to hang on over the next 5.2 miles and finish within the top 20, thus taking home the $250 award. Incredibly, he did it! He was leading by mere inches at the mile mark and had to run a ridiculous 4:10 to do it! He managed to hang on over those next 5.2 hilly miles, finishing 17th and earning that $250. To this day, he recalls that as being one of the most painful running experiences of his life.

Lucciana Rodriguez

Anya Joshi, Julia Boucher, Lily Gamino

CHAPTER THREE

Tuck In!

Maybe you are a NASCAR fan? Maybe you've watched the Tour-de-France? Have you ever noticed the degree to which one driver or rider tries to tuck in behind another? They are obsessive about it. There's a reason. For those of you who live in the northern parts of the country, you've surely seen Canadian Geese flying in their famous "V" formation. They are not doing this just to impress the humans on the ground far below. There is a science behind it and a distinct physical advantage to be gained by doing so.

As I mentioned earlier, I am neither a physicist nor an engineer. I am smart enough to avoid getting into a lengthy, detailed conversation about aerodynamics. I'll leave those details to people who are far smarter than I am. For those of you who care to do any additional reading on this subject, you'll likely find studies suggesting that a car, a bike rider, or a goose who is able to tuck in close behind another is going to burn as much as eight percent less energy than is his or her leading counterpart. Eight percent is a lot!

Rather than running alongside a fellow competitor for several hundred meters during the course of a 5K or even allowing him or her to tuck in behind you, this 8% equation suggests to me that you'd be far better served by tucking in behind him or her for a bit. Let them break the wind for a while. Even if this 8% estimate were somehow proven to be statistically inaccurate to the high side, a mere 2 or 3% advantage is still well worth capitalizing upon.

If you were to watch a flock of Canadian Geese fly for an extended period of time, you would notice that at some point, the leader, the one who has been at the front of the "V," breaking the wind for everyone else, would eventually yield that leadership role to another goose and that he or she would assume a spot further back in the formation. Why? Because it is easier.

Taking this concept one step further, forget about the aerodynamic part of the equation for a minute. There's a lot more to it than that. If we are competing against one another in a 5K and you have tucked in behind me, not only am I now the one breaking the wind and expending as much as 8% more energy, I can't see you. From a psychological perspective, that is unnerving. Where are you? Are you fading behind me? Are you getting ready to blow past me at any point? Anything that distracts me from the task at hand, that is, running to the best of my ability and maintaining maximal focus, is going to work to your benefit.

Here, however, is an important word of caution related to this "tuck in" concept. Don't get lazy and complacent. Unless you are near the front of the pack, tucking in for an indefinite period of time is rarely a good race strategy. Short term? Yes. Indefinitely? Probably not. Suppose that I have effectively tucked in behind you for the past 800 or 1000 meters. I am expending a bit less energy and my mere presence is probably distracting you. Maybe though, you have begun to fade. The runners ahead of us have begun to pull away and the runners behind us are steadily gaining ground. I need to be monitoring our status constantly. Perhaps you are effectively pulling us both along to a faster finish time or, conversely, maybe you are fading and I, as a direct result of being focused solely on tucking in behind you, am now beginning to fade as well. There comes a time in that case, where I will need to go around you, allowing you to fall off if that is what is going to happen.

Lily Thomas at the FHSAA 2A District 6 Championship. Photo courtesy of Mark Stonecipher and fl.milesplit.com

CHAPTER FOUR

Overcoming Obstacles

It would be great if it were always partly cloudy, wind-free, and 60 degrees on race day but it rarely is. It would be great if every course was flat, dry, and well maintained. They rarely are. Depending upon where you live, you may encounter excessive heat, cold, hills, rain, snow, and wind from meet to meet. To what degree are you, as a runner, going to be able to deal with, and block out these outside variables? If it is windy, it is windy for everyone and not just for you. If it is cold, it is equally cold for everyone. In the case of an excessively hilly course, the hills are there for everyone to deal with equally.

There is no doubt that some people are better hill runners than others. It is a fact that some people handle the heat better than others. Perhaps the wind is going to more negatively affect a runner weighing 90 pounds than it would one weighing 160 but it is going to be an annoyance for all regardless. These are all recognized, common norms of the human condition. You've likely heard the term "mental toughness" used as it applies to athletes from various sports. There have been countless books written on this very subject. Specific to distance running, we can view mental toughness, in part, as our ability to block out negative influences and to deal with the conditions that we have been dealt on any given day.

Are there certain outside influences that tend to affect you more negatively than others as a runner? How are you going to respond the next time you encounter those conditions at a meet, whether it be cold, hills, wind, or rain?

I will conclude this very brief chapter with a quick, topic-appropriate anecdote. . . . During the fall of my junior year in high school, we had a dual meet scheduled with one of our big cross-town rivals. It was unusually warm for early September. The other school's top runner was a year ahead of me in school and he and I had gone back and forth over the past couple of years. He would beat me on occasion and vice-versa. Paul and I would oftentimes talk for a while before any given meet. On this particular day, he was really focused on the heat. He talked about how slow it was going to be and even went so far as to suggest that they should consider cancelling the meet all together. I nodded my head as if in full agreement, knowing that on this particular day, the race was essentially already over.

Relative to my competition, I'd always found that the heat affected me less than it did most others. Sure, I was likely to run a bit slower under excessively hot conditions but probably not to the same degree as many of the other runners. In this case, Paul was already beaten. He was way too focused on the adverse weather situation and not nearly focused enough on the task at hand - running to his best ability on that particular day. That is exactly how that meet played out. He was never really a factor in the race and we won rather handily.

This side note before we move on . . . the heat is no joke. Respect it. We'll talk more about this later.

Hayden Nason (#784, above) and Lauren Lappin (#783, below) - Torrential rains and several inches of standing water greeted those participating in the 2023 AAU National Championship Meet held in Tallahassee, Florida.

Talk about overcoming obstacles! Notice that Charlie Bevan (Top) has lost his left shoe at some point during this race. He still managed to PR! On the bottom, Thomas O'Brien, Lauren Lappin, and Emma Garner at the soaking wet AAU National Championships Meet.

CHAPTER FIVE

Personal Records

Breaking records doesn't come easily for most of us. Records are records for a reason after all, whether we are talking about school records, state records, or even world records. One of the great things about our sport, however, is that personal records are there for all of us to attain. PRs are a big deal. They tell us that we are doing something right and that all of our hard work is not being done in vain.

The newer that we are to the sport, the more frequently we are likely to find ourselves running a personal record. So too is the likelihood greater that those PRs will be sizeable: 45 seconds, a minute, two minutes. As we continue to improve, however, PRs will likely occur less frequently and when they do happen, it may only be by a few seconds each time. That's normal. That's the way it is supposed to work.

I frequently tell my student-athletes about my own 5K PR. Specifically, the fact that I set it as a collegiate sophomore and did not break it again until halfway through my senior season. Two years! Even then, I broke it by a mere seven seconds. I have student-athletes who get upset when they don't set a PR every weekend. If only it was that easy.

Improvement as a runner is not a linear progression. That is, you are not necessarily going to run faster week to week to week. You may find significant peaks and valleys along the way. Is it likely that you are running faster at the end of the season than at the beginning? Is it likely that you are running faster as a senior than you were as a sophomore? Yes and yes. Neither is a guarantee however. There are so many variables at play. Variables including injuries and training habits that we will address going forward. Try to avoid the natural and understandable tendency to become frustrated when you've not run a PR in a while. That's normal.

Weather considerations, the level of competition, and course variations are among the issues that play a role in determining how fast you are likely to run on any given weekend. It is entirely possible that your "best" race of the season may not be your fastest.

Different coaches have different means by which they recognize PRs and there really is no right or wrong answer. Here is what I have done over the past several years. . . . Many of the larger collegiate football programs award school-logo helmet stickers to their players week to week for having made exceptional plays during a game, whether it be scoring a touchdown, intercepting a pass, or recovering a fumble. By the end of any given season, it is not uncommon to see a player from Michigan, Ohio State or Florida State, among others, with a helmet sporting 20-25 such logo stickers. Following that concept, I developed "PR pins," simple buttons with the school logo on them. On the first practice following any given meet, we begin by awarding a pin to any of our runners who may have set a PR the day before. It has quickly become a much-anticipated tradition. There is nothing better than seeing one of my runners in the hallways at school with four or five PR pins proudly attached to his or her backpack.

Personal Records and School Records are big deals. As coaches,
we need to make every effort to recognize and honor both.
PR pins and personalized, engraved relay batons.

CHAPTER SIX

Scheduling – From a Coach's Perspective

A couple of quick paragraphs on the topic of scheduling meets... As is true with so many other running-related topics, there is no one singular right or wrong answer as to the perfect number of meets during a season. There are a variety of variables to consider. Is your team especially young and inexperienced? Are you anticipating being highly competitive or not so much? Do budgeting and travel considerations come into play? Are there certain meets in which you are required or expected to participate? Has your state, county, or league established minimum or maximum meet expectations?

From experience, I have found that seven or eight regular season meets prior to any post-season competition is probably the maximum. Additionally, I've found that offering a couple of weekends off during the season reaps considerable rewards, both mental and physical, for the student-athletes as individuals and for the program as a whole. Asking a 15 or 16-year-old to be ready to compete at a high level more than six, seven, or eight times during the course of a regular season oftentimes seems to lead to burnout and injuries by the end of the year. I've seen that with other teams as recently as this past fall. Maybe you consider designating one of those meets as being solely a "JV" meet, allowing those kids who might not be competing in the postseason the opportunity to run as varsity athletes for a change?

Of those seven or eight regular season meets, I will commonly designate only three or four of them as being true "focus" meets, meets in which we want to be sharp, fresh, and ready to run at our very best.

I have found, as you probably have too, that scheduling a meet for each and every weekend during the season makes planning workouts and recovery days all that much more difficult. I work hard to schedule around homecoming weekend and those Saturdays on which SATs or ACTs may be scheduled.

Prior to having reported to college for my freshman cross country season, I remember receiving our meet schedule for that fall. I saw only three meets listed prior to the SEC Championships. I turned the page over. Nope, that was it, three meets. I'd been used to nine or ten meets per season during my high school years.

Collegiate cross country, especially at the Division 1 level, is a completely different animal. Rather than running your weekly 5K, you are now running 6K, 8K, or even 10K and there can be an extensive amount of travel involved. The intensity and volume of your workouts is commonly higher than what you experienced during high school and it would be wholly unrealistic and irresponsible to schedule eight or nine meets during the course of the regular season.

Braden Turner at the FHSAA 2A Region 3 Championships.
Photo courtesy of Mark Stonecipher and fl.milesplit.com

CHAPTER SEVEN

Don't Do Anything "Weird"

Towards the end of any given cross country season, the student-athletes that I'm working with know that the "Don't Do Anything Weird" conversation is coming soon. The regular season is winding down. You've had good meets and perhaps a clunker or two along the way. You've made mistakes in meets from time to time and, hopefully, have learned from those mistakes. The postseason is now at hand: conference championships, districts, regionals, and states. Maybe nationals? Now is not the time for experimentation. Now is not the time for making any major adjustments to how you approach a meet. Now is not the time to do anything "weird."

When I was a junior in high school, we had a very good cross country team. We were strong up front, our depth was good, even our number six and seven runners were capable of displacing the opposing team's fourth and fifth runners from time to time. By late October, we were still undefeated. One of our crosstown rival schools was also having a good season. They too were undefeated. We were scheduled to run against each other as part of a big meet one Saturday morning. Though it was not a championship meet, we were focused and ready to go.

At about 800 meters into the race, I looked around to take inventory of those runners who were around me. It was all of the usual suspects. Nothing unexpected. Nothing unexpected, except . . . there on my right shoulder was one of my teammates, a kid named Doug. Doug was usually our number three or four runner. He was an important piece of our team puzzle that fall but surely had no business being among the race leaders a half mile into the race. Surely he was a smarter runner than this strategy would suggest? "Doug . . . what are you doing?" I asked him as discretely as possible considering the circumstances. "Hey Rankin," he replied, "You know those bear-shaped things of honey that you always see at the grocery store? I just pounded one of those. I feel unbelievable!" Well, of course, he felt unbelievable. Honey is essentially nature's rocket fuel, sugar in its purest form. The problem is that, much like rocket fuel, the energy that honey provides is fleeting and the "sugar crash" that follows can be enormous. That's what happened to Doug on that particular day. Among the leaders at 800 meters, he was essentially crawling by the two-mile mark. Opposing runners were passing him as though he was standing still. Ultimately we lost that meet by a single point. While I appreciate Doug's enthusiasm and wanting to run his best on that particular day, drinking a big thing of honey just prior to the start of the race definitely qualifies as something "weird." Did we lose that meet as a direct result of Doug's ill-conceived honey-based race strategy that morning? Probably. We'll never know for sure.

This notion of wanting to avoid approaching a big meet in an unusual, untested manner extends far beyond Doug and his honey.

It can relate to race strategy. If, over the course of the season, you have established that you are best served by going out in a 6:30 first mile, why would you suddenly decide to go out in 6:05 now that you're running in the district meet?

It can relate to diet. You've likely experimented and learned what to eat the night before, and morning of, your meets. Why would you alter those tried and true patterns and risk negative consequences as you prepare for the conference championships?

It can relate to your gear. It's tempting to break out a new pair of spikes for the big regional championship meet. Don't do it. You've run well in that older pair of spikes all season. They will make it for one more meet. Don't risk blisters or other footwear-related issues by wearing a brand new pair of spikes for the first time simply because you're running in a more meaningful meet.

I could have just as easily entitled this mini-chapter "Don't Do Anything Different." While Doug's honey idea surely qualifies as "weird," these other scenarios really don't. They are perhaps merely "different" rather than "weird."

The bottom line is this. . . . If you feel the need to experiment with your gear, your diet, your race strategy, do so during the regular season when the meets may not be quite as important. The postseason is not a time for experimentation.

I'll commonly bring this guy along to those late-season team meetings as a reminder. . . . "Now is not the time to do anything 'weird'!"

CHAPTER EIGHT

Weight Room?

Opinions tend to vary considerably when it comes to distance runners and the amount of time that they need to spend in the weight room. Are there potential benefits? Absolutely, but there are a lot of things to consider.

The need to prioritize correctly and to establish a proper balance - running versus strength training - is very real. On more than one occasion, I have had a young runner approach me about the possibility of doing some additional work in the weight room every few days, seemingly convinced that it will help his or her running. They're right, it probably would. To what degree, however, is that young runner addressing the basics of our sport, focusing on building his or her mileage, limiting the number of days that he or she takes off, finishing his or her workouts consistently? If the runner in question is only running three or four times per week, it would make a lot more sense to focus on building that up to five or six days per week before worrying about trying to squeeze in some time in the weight room. The added benefits resulting from increasing his or her running workload week to week will far outweigh anything that he or she might be able to gain by visiting the weight room every other day. Essentially, I view the weight room this way - make sure that you are executing A, B, and C properly before you worry about moving on to D, E, and F. My apologies to those who love the weights, but for a distance runner, while it surely has a place as part of a well-balanced training program, the weight room is not priority number one.

As I did above, rather than referring specifically to the "weight room," perhaps we are all better served by thinking of it in terms of "strength training". For the most part, after all, the type of strength training from which a distance runner is going to benefit the most is not dependent upon a weight room at all. Think along the lines of body-weight type of exercises: planks, sit-ups, push-ups, calf raises, walking lunges. Exercises such as these don't require a weight room at all and can be done in a relatively limited amount of time.

In an ideal world, we would have an infinite amount of time during which to conduct practice every day. We would have plenty of time to hit the weight room after practice two or three times per week. That's not reality, however. For those who are wholly committed to the weight room, be careful that it does not come at the expense of your running time. We are, after all, runners who lift weights, not weight lifters who run.

I recently had one of my student-athletes approach me with big news from the weight room. "Coach, coach, I just bench-pressed 190!" Though I did my best to share in his excitement and surely wish that I too was capable of benching 190 pounds, my silent response to his excited announcement was "Why?"

This is not new news to most of us. As distance runners, we are endurance-focused beings. Our weight room/strength training work should be focused on lighter weights and higher repetitions. Rather than benching 190 pounds a single time, I'd much prefer and suggest that the young man in question attempt a couple of sets of 10–12 repetitions at a more manageable 100–120 pounds.

To be sure, a variety of lightweight strength training exercises can be, and frequently are, used as part of the injury recovery and prevention process. Many of the most common injuries that we encounter as distance runners can be prevented and/or resolved via these means. We'll touch briefly upon injury issues later. In the meantime, if I come across as being "anti-weight room," I assure you that that's not the case but please jump back a few paragraphs and reread what I had to say about prioritization and balance.

CHAPTER NINE

When the Going Gets Tough

Having been around this sport for as long as I have been, I've long since learned what a humbling sport it can be. It can break your heart. There are guaranteed to be plenty of disappointments. Those times when you lose a race by a fraction of a second. Those times when you miss qualifying for regionals by one place. Those championship meets where you come up just short of making the medal stand. I've been there both as a runner and as a coach, countless times. It's tough sometimes. Really tough. I would suggest, however, that it is these tough times from which we stand to learn the most as runners. Moreover, I would suggest that these tough times make the good times all that much more special.

Two years ago, in addition to coaching my own high school's teams, I was working with a local 8th grade girl who had shown a tremendous amount of upside potential as a runner. She went undefeated throughout the entirety of her fall season only to finish third at her league championship meet, losing to two girls whom she'd beaten with relative ease three or four times during the course of the regular season. It was crushing, for both of us. There were tears, hers as well as my own. All I could do was assure Addie that better things lay ahead and that we would get through it together. Exactly a year later, I reminded her of that promise moments after she, now a high school freshman, had lead our team in a state-qualifying effort, a first for our program in nearly 20 years.

How you respond to those negative, tough-to-take situations that are bound to present themselves from time to time during your running career is going to go a long way towards determining your ultimate level of success.

Before moving on to other topics, I want to share another brief story with you. While this story is about me in a literal sense, it really isn't. As a senior in high school, I had a pretty good cross country season. We had a home meet against one of our league rivals one Thursday afternoon that September. Frankly, they weren't very good that year. I won the meet and, if my memory serves me correctly, we took four or five of the top six places. Not long after the meet had concluded, I'd found my way to a nearby picnic table to remove my spikes and drink a little water. From where I was sitting, I could hear one of my teammates, a kid named Jeff, talking to one of our assistant coaches. Jeff wasn't much of a runner but that's not an integral part of this story. Neither Jeff nor the coach were aware that I was eavesdropping.

"Did Kyle win again?" I heard Jeff ask our coach.

"Yes," the coach answered.

"Kyle always wins," Jeff replied, sounding almost as if he wished that I hadn't.

"Well, you're right, Jeff, Kyle has won a lot lately but remember, he's also lost more races than anyone you've ever known."

Wow. Think about that for a moment. The coach was in no way speaking of me in a disparaging manner. Facts are facts and that was a fact. This can be a tough sport. It can really test your resolve sometimes.

Be tough, be resilient, and be prepared to handle those challenging times when they inevitably come around.

Addie Gurick: A Conference and District champion as a freshman and the very definition of the word "coachable."

CHAPTER TEN

Gaining a Psychological Advantage

There are very few guarantees in this crazy sport of ours but I am going to share one with you right now. One that, hopefully, you can use to your advantage again and again.

Let's say that you've reached the two-mile mark of a grueling 5K. By this point, you are physically and psychologically ready for it to be over. It's no longer fun and the "pain meter" is cranked way up. You've reached the crest of a sizeable hill and your body just wants to shut down. One of your fellow competitors has been running beside you for the past 1,000 meters. As bad as you are feeling at this point, you can't help but assume that he or she is feeling better than you are. How could they possibly feel any worse? Here is the guarantee . . . at that very moment he or she is thinking the exact same thing about you. It's human nature. The challenge now becomes, knowing what you know, what can you do to convince them that you are, in fact, feeling better than they are, even though you surely are not?

Sometimes merely having a teammate with you is enough to distract, frustrate, and discourage an opposing competitor. There are two of you and only one of them. Even in complete silence, that can spook an opposing runner. What if you and your teammate are able to converse? "Good job, John, that mile was 5:55. Let's go." The mere fact that you are able to communicate with your teammate in this manner might be enough to rattle your opposition. To be clear, sportsmanship, of course, comes above all else. You never want to initiate any physical contact nor speak derisively to a competitor, whether during a race or afterwards.

What if you were to throw in a 30-meter surge at the top of that hill? Is it going to be painful? Absolutely! But it is also likely to shake your competition. You've managed to open up a ten meter gap and now he or she is suddenly much more interested in who is coming up behind them and has essentially given up on maintaining pace with you.

Here is something to avoid at nearly all costs, and it is something that I've seen many, many times over the years. Halfway through a race, as you near your coach or perhaps a parent, you feel the need to share your pain with them. "Coach, I can't breathe," "Coach, my knee is killing me," "Coach, I am cramping bad." All of those things may be true but you need to resist the urge to audibilize them. You've just alerted your competition as to your weakened state. You've just played a card that you didn't need to play, likely giving them a renewed sense of confidence and a sense as to how vulnerable you may be over that last mile of the race.

My advice is this… Think about what an opposing runner might be able to do to convince you that they are feeling pretty good even though they surely aren't. Then, within the guidelines of good sportsmanship, do it to them instead.

Leg speed to spare: Braden Turner ran a 2:02 800 as a freshman, one of the fastest times posted by an FHSAA 9th grader during the 2022 season. Olivia Boncelet PRed in the 1,600 on three consecutive weekends.

CHAPTER ELEVEN

Heat and Hydration

I spoke about heat-related issues very briefly earlier but it is a topic that deserves revisiting. Heat and humidity can be deadly. I encourage my student-athletes not to fear the heat but to absolutely respect it and to be aware of how dangerous it can be.

Above all else, stay hydrated! Keep in mind that it takes a while for your body to absorb fluids. If you realize that you may be a bit dehydrated at 2:00 p.m., the odds of you being fully hydrated and ready to go by the time practice starts at 3:00 p.m. are very slim. Your body can only absorb fluids at a certain rate. Drinking a liter of water at 2:00 p.m. is not going to rehydrate you quite the way you think it might by the time that practice starts. Several ounces of water per hour, every hour will prove to be much more beneficial. Plan accordingly. Hydrate throughout the day.

Energy drinks and sodas are really not viable alternatives in terms of hydration and running. Water is your best alternative, especially prior to running. Some of the electrolyte-enhanced drinks (Gatorade, PowerAde) may be beneficial following a particularly grueling workout but when in doubt, you can't go wrong with good, old-fashioned water.

Your ability to perform at your optimum level is lessened considerably when you are dehydrated, but this is about much more than performance; this is about your safety and health.

Again, I am not a doctor but the concept here is fairly simple. Our bodies cool themselves via perspiration and the evaporation thereof. Perspiration is dependent upon fluid intake and absorption.

High humidity limits the degree to which our sweat evaporates, thus limiting our body's ability to cool itself. An 80 degree day with high humidity can be every bit as dangerous as can a relatively dry 90 degree day.

Having coached in southern Florida for the past several years, we hold practices at 5:00 a.m. and 6:00 p.m. simply to avoid the heat and humidity of the midafternoon. Seriously, 5:00 a.m. It's that serious an issue.

Wear lighter clothes when possible. Run in shady areas. Run in areas that are likely to be exposed to the wind. Modify your pace a bit if necessary.

In all of my years as a coach, I consider myself lucky to have had only three instances in which one of my student-athletes had heat-related issues. All three were relatively minor and resolved themselves fairly quickly but they were all scary for me as a coach and undoubtedly even scarier for the kids involved. What I find interesting is that all three of those instances took place when I was coaching up north on days when the temperatures were in the upper 70s and lower 80s. The likely reason? In southern Florida, it is seemingly always hot. The heat and humidity is never going to surprise you nor sneak up on you. A certain degree of acclimatization has likely taken place for most of us. We've been taught about heat, humidity, and hydration. That's not always true in the more northern parts of the country. Be aware, be careful, and be willing to make any necessary adjustments to your running schedule.

If at any point you feel those common characteristics of heat-related issues (chills, a cessation of sweating, confusion, extreme fatigue or lethargy, dizziness), don't try to be a hero, just stop. Get some water. Get in the shade. Get indoors.

Just getting started. Hudson Casto is one of the brightest young distance-running stars of south Florida.

CHAPTER TWELVE

Diet and Nutrition

I need to be careful here, because, when it comes to diet, this is one of those "do as I say, not as I do" topics. I've always tended to be a picky eater, grossly undervaluing fruits and vegetables as part of my diet. It has not been until more recently that I have come to realize and appreciate how truly important one's diet can be. Not only in terms of weight control but also as it applies to energy levels and overall health and fitness. You've probably heard the old adage "you are what you eat." Well, yeah.

My biggest vice had always been soda: Pepsi, 7Up, Dr. Pepper. The truth is that beverages like these really have nothing to offer other than a tremendous amount of sugar and a lot of empty calories. More and more, modern science is suggesting how bad excessive amounts of sugar may really be for us.

Focus on trying to achieve a balanced diet. "Everything in moderation," as they say. If you are interested in learning more about the various food groups, vitamins, and which foods to focus on and perhaps which to avoid, there are a wide variety of books available on diet and nutrition for athletes in general and runners more specifically. I'm not going to pretend to be something I'm not by delving any deeper into nutritional science within the pages of this book.

Everyone is different. You may need to take on a certain amount of "trial and error" as you learn what best suits your running needs from a nutritional standpoint. Are you one of those runners who prefers not to eat anything on the morning of a big meet? Maybe a half a banana, some water, and piece of toast three hours beforehand is what works best for you? Experiment a little but don't wait until the morning of that big meet to do so.

Early rough drafts of this book included a "Diet and Nutrition" subchapter on "Carbo-Loading" - the idea that eating copious amounts of carbohydrates as a leadup to a big competition will help your performance. The idea has some merit but its upside potential is really very limited in the degree to which it might help someone running a 5K. Those benefits are much more likely to be enjoyed by one running much greater distances, typically those which take a minimum of 45 minutes.

As I began wading deeper and deeper into the carbo-loading concept, I could feel many of you beginning to fade. I could feel myself beginning to fade. For some, conversations about ATP and the body's burning of glucose probably too closely resemble those never-ending lectures that you have to endure during 4th period science class. I will spare you for now.

The bottom line is this when it comes to the concept of carbo-loading. . . . Is carbo-loading likely to do us any harm? No. Nor, however, is it likely to yield much of an appreciable benefit over the course of a 5K.

One final, random thought on carbo-loading. . . . There are dieticians and scientists who are now suggesting that for carbo-loading to truly be of benefit to a given endurance athlete, he or she must first go through a carbo-depletion process. The theory holds that the human body, sensing a scarcity of carbohydrates, will then overcompensate by storing more than it normally would when the carbs are suddenly reintroduced to our diet within a few days of our competition.

CHAPTER THIRTEEN

Don't Look Back!

We've all seen it. Most of us are guilty of having done it. It is the tendency to look over our shoulder during that last few hundred meters of a given race, oftentimes repeatedly, to see where our competition is. Are they gaining on us? Have they fallen behind? I get it. You've just run yourself through a grueling first 2.9 miles of a 5K race, and whether you're in 1st place or 101st place, the thought of being passed at the finish line is tough to deal with. This natural tendency to want to look back to see what is going on behind us is seemingly much more common among younger runners than it is among older ones but it happens at every level. There are at least three reasons as to why I, as a coach, encourage resisting that natural temptation to take a peek back over your shoulder during the final stages of your race.

1. **Look where you are going.** During my sophomore year in college, the NCAA Division 1 National Championship meet was hosted by the University of Arizona. The men's and women's races were both run on a nicely manicured golf course on the outskirts of Tucson. On the men's side, Joe Falcon from the University of Arkansas was widely considered to be the favorite that year. I don't recall him having lost a meet all season.

With several hundred meters to go in the men's 10K, Joe, who was leading at the time, uncharacteristically glanced over his shoulder to see where his closest rival was (Aaron Ramirez from the University of Northern Arizona). As he did so, he stepped on a sprinkler head and fell down. Ramirez seized the opportunity, quickly taking the lead from Falcon. Joe was not injured and he quickly got back on his feet but the damage was done. Ramirez was the NCAA Champion.

2. **You're costing yourself valuable time.** Let's assume that it only costs you a tenth of a second every time that you look over your shoulder to check on your competition. (It's probably a little bit more than that). Admittedly, a tenth of a second is rarely a big deal over the course of a 5K, but let's now say that you glance over your shoulder five or six or seven times during the course of that last 600 meters. You've just cost yourself nearly a full second. We have all either beaten someone or been beaten by someone in a race by a second or less at some point in our running careers. It happens a lot more than one might think. Wouldn't it just make more sense to run that last 600 meters as if somebody were right on your shoulder? Maybe they are, maybe they're not. Run your hardest. If they pass you, you can take solace in knowing that you did everything that you could do to hold them off. If it turns out that there was nobody right behind you in the first place, you've likely just run a second or two faster than you might have otherwise. Nothing wrong with that.

3. **You're telling your competition that you are worried and that you are not confident in your own abilities over that final stretch of the race.** This is perhaps the single most important reason as to why you should try to avoid looking

over your shoulder as you near the finish line. Let's assume that I have been a steady 30 meters behind you during the middle portion of our 5K. I just can't seem to close the gap. As we near that final stretch, I have perhaps subconsciously begun to give up. Suddenly, I see you looking over your shoulder. By doing so, you are telling me that you may be in trouble, that you may be vulnerable, and that you are questioning your own ability to stay ahead of me as the finish line approaches. My interest and determination is suddenly renewed. Whether I catch you or not remains to be seen but I am suddenly fully reinvested *in trying to do so.*

A runner who glances over his or her shoulder to see where you are will almost assuredly do so a second time, and then a third. Usually over the same shoulder. As the trailing runner, I want to try to take advantage of this perceived vulnerability to the best of my ability. Supposing that he or she has now glanced back over their left shoulder to see where I am two or three times. I know that they are going to do it again. Perhaps I try to position myself just off of their right shoulder, anticipating that next left-shoulder glance. When they look, I surge past them on the blind side. Suddenly, their greatest fear, the thing that they had been guarding against in the first place, has become a reality.

Madison Tillman: Competitive and passionate, I had the pleasure of coaching Madison throughout her high school years in Pennsylvania. She went on to run at Ursinus College.

CHAPTER FOURTEEN

Don't Look Back – Part Two

Related to that natural tendency to want to look back to monitor your competition, as I said, I get it. There's a certain comfort in knowing whether your lead is a meter, five meters, or twenty meters. But if we agree that looking over our shoulder might not be the best idea, how then are we supposed to know who is behind us and how far back they are? Here are a few tricks. . . .

1. Shadows. On a track, the sun will be at your back at least once per lap, assuming that the sun is out and that it's not high noon. In cross country, the sun's constant presence is less dependable but you can oftentimes glance down, perhaps to your left or to your right, to determine how close your competition is behind you based upon their shadows.

2. You can hear them. You can hear them breathing. You can hear them spit. You can hear their spikes in the gravel.

3. You can hear their coaches or parents shouting words of encouragement. Several seconds of silence after you have passed should suggest to you that you have a decent lead over the runner behind you.

4. When rounding a 90 degree turn you can oftentimes get a feel for who is behind you out of the corner of our eye.

5. If you are running near any buildings you can sometimes see their reflections in the windows.

6. If you hear the crowd yelling "Go Olivia, go Anisa" as you enter that last straightaway but your name is Victoria, you can assume that you've got company nearby. Listen for that kind of thing.

Several years ago, while still coaching at the high school level in Pennsylvania, I was fortunate to have a pair of twin brothers, Chase and Jack Balick, leading our cross country team. They were both great kids and very talented runners. One of our biggest crosstown rivals had a similarly talented runner named Jeffrey. As might be expected, Jack and Chase always wanted to know where Jeffrey was throughout the entirety of any cross country race. If he was ahead of them, presumably they could see him. If he was behind them, however, it became a little trickier for them to know exactly where he was. In those instances, when Jack and Chase would pass me, I would, of course, yell words of encouragement. But in the interest of letting those two know exactly where Jeffrey was, I took to yelling out words of encouragement to him as well. "Good job, Jack, good job, Chase . . . way to go, Jeffrey." They knew to listen for Jeffrey's name and were able to figure out exactly how far behind them he was without ever having to look around.

Whether on the track or cross country course, Jack Balick's (#2) leg speed graded out to a "10." If he was near the leaders with 300 meters to go, I could just walk away, knowing that the race was essentially over. Jack went on to run at the University of Pittsburgh.

Highly coachable and a great example of what it takes to be a team captain, Chase Balick (#5 on top, #7 on bottom) went on to run at Syracuse University.

CHAPTER FIFTEEN

Warming Up and Cooling Down

Experience has taught me that younger runners oftentimes have a better comprehension of the need for a proper warmup than they do of the need for a proper cooldown. Here are a few random thoughts on both. . . .

A proper warmup is especially important on those days on which you are going to be running hard. It prepares the body for the rigors that lie ahead. Muscles that are warm and loose are significantly less prone to injury than are those which are relatively cold and inflexible. So too are they likely to function more smoothly and efficiently. You wouldn't jump into your car and immediately slam the accelerator to the floor without expecting negative repercussions. Don't do that to your own body.

A good warmup routine doesn't need to take a half an hour. That sort of time frame might be more reasonable for a shot putter or a sprinter.

We want to avoid performing five or six stretches for a singular muscle group while neglecting the others all together.

A well-proportioned blend of "static" stretches and "dynamic" warmup activities has become the accepted norm over the past twenty years. Static stretches, like the traditional wall-stretch for your calves and Achilles tendons, are those which include very little, if any, movement. Dynamic warm up activities might include bounding drills or the ever popular "Mock A" and "Mock B" drills.

An argument can easily be made in favor of establishing a specific warmup routine for practice every single day. Many of us stand to benefit from that type of structure and routine. There are those who might argue that given muscle groups stand to benefit the most from a stretching routine that is performed in a nearly identical manner from day to day, five or six days per week. Perhaps. On the other hand, does our warmup routine on a day on which we are going out for an easy eight miles need to be quite as extensive as it does on a day on which we are going to be doing repeat 400s? Probably not. Time is limited and valuable. On those easy distance days, there is no need for the amount of time that we spend warming up to be equal to the amount of time that we spend actually running. If need be, take that first half mile of your run a little slower to assure that you have warmed up enough.

You'll notice that I have intentionally avoided including countless photos of various stretching exercises within the pages of this publication. Perhaps that is for a later edition. Keep it simple, keep it focused, and make it purposeful.

Here is the part of the warmup and cooldown equation that many young runners seem to struggle with. . . . In our chapter on proper pacing we talked briefly about the body's creation of lactate. Again, I am using "lactate" as an all-encompassing reference to the "exhaust" that our body creates when work is performed at any level. Lactate is a byproduct of your muscles having performed work just as a car's exhaust is a byproduct of its combustion engine having fired. I realize that I am being a bit repetitive here but I feel that it's appropriate in the context of developing an understanding of why a proper cooldown can be so important.

The body works to rid itself of lactate as quickly as it can. The harder we are running, the more lactate our muscles are producing. Heading out for a relatively easy six or seven mile run, it is not unrealistic to expect that a well-trained body might be able to rid itself of nearly 100% of the lactate that it is producing just as quickly as it is being produced while we run. There is essentially no accumulation of lactate at all in this case as we are operating well below what we previously referred to as being our "lactate threshold." I've been puzzled on many occasions by that runner who returns to campus at the end of a long, easy run only to take a few sips of water and then embark on a short "cooldown" run. What are they cooling down from exactly? Had this been a more aggressive fartlek or tempo run, perhaps a few minutes of easy jogging might make sense. As it stands, however, based on the assumption of an easy six or seven mile run, as suggested above, there is really nothing to "cool down" from per se. If you'd like to add on an extra half mile or so, great. Otherwise, you're good. Spend a few easy minutes stretching, get some water, maybe throw in a few striders, and you're done.

Conversely, on a day when we are running 10 × 400 meters with a 2 minute recovery in between each, our bodies are producing a tremendous amount of lactate. The two-minute recovery is hardly enough time for the body to catch up and clear itself of all of this muscular waste, nor is it intended to be. By the time our workout is over, we are fatigued and our bodies are way behind in terms on restoring normal lactate levels. That process is ongoing but can take many hours depending upon the intensity of our workout and our own level of physical conditioning.

In these cases, you are doing yourself a gross disservice by just stopping, taking off your spikes, and heading home. You can greatly increase the rate at which your body eliminates all of its excess muscular waste by going for an easy cooldown jog of as little as five to ten minutes. A slightly elevated heart rate, a warmer body temperature, and some light jogging are going to help speed this process up considerably.

Have you ever competed in a meet or run a particularly hard workout and then immediately just jumped in the car for the long ride home? Were you surprised by how stiff and uncomfortable you felt when you got home and tried to get out of the car? Now you know why. Had you taken those extra few minutes to cool down properly, you would likely have felt much better when you got home and the recovery process would have been that much further along.

Taylor Morrison at the FHSAA 2A District 6 Championship.
Photo courtesy of Mark Stonecipher and fl.milesplit.com

CHAPTER SIXTEEN

Strengths and Weaknesses

We all have strengths and weaknesses, both as runners and as human beings. Specific to running, the degree to which we are able to identify our own strengths and weaknesses will go a long way towards determining our ultimate success as runners. As coaches, it may be unrealistic for us to expect a young runner to be able to be self-analytical enough to determine his or own strengths and weaknesses. It is oftentimes a process best undertaken in tandem.

Some young runners are better hill runners than others. Some have greater closing leg speed. Still others seem to have much better endurance than do their counterparts. This is normal. The challenge comes in being able to identify and address those strengths and weaknesses.

A generation ago, coaching philosophy at that time suggested focusing on and addressing a given runner's weaknesses rather than their strengths. Modern training philosophy, however, suggests the exact opposite. Once you have successfully identified a given distance runner's strengths, work to maximize and make the most of whatever that strength might be.

As an example, suppose that I have a 9th grade runner whom we'll call "Hannah." Hannah seemingly has exceptional endurance. She enjoys those longer runs and commonly leaves her teammates behind on those seven and eight mile days. When it comes to leg speed, however, yikes. Hannah really struggles to get her legs moving over the course of 200 or 400 meters and is seemingly always at the back of the pack during those types of workouts.

Were this 1975, we would likely address this issue by having Hannah run workouts of 200 -300 - 400 meters several times per week, attempting to address what is very clearly her glaring weakness as a runner. That's not what modern training philosophy nor my own experience and training as a runner and coach suggests, however.

It is important that we have identified Hannah's weakness as a runner. In this case, it was relatively easy. Our challenge now as a coach and as a two-person team, runner and coach, is to work on developing and maximizing her strength, that is, her endurance. Endurance is her natural advantage and it is what is going to most enable her to be successful as she develops as a runner. If she is to win championships and set records, it is going to be largely because of her remarkable endurance and not because of her middling leg speed.

To be clear, we are not completely ignoring those leg speed concerns. By no means are we turning a blind eye to the issue. Neither are we making it our sole focus, assuming that her natural tendency towards endurance will continue to just keep developing on its own. Priority one is identifying and working to maximize a young runner's strengths.

I will very often pose the following hypothetical question to my distance kids. . . . "Suppose that you were running in a cross country meet. With 500 or 600 meters to go, you are running right alongside

100 similarly talented runners." Remember this is hypothetical. "Of those 100 similarly talented runners, how many are you going to outkick to the finish line versus how many are likely to outkick you?"

At an absolutely minimum, a question like this is likely to get them thinking about themselves in terms of strengths and weaknesses, in terms of leg speed versus endurance. Similar questions can be asked about hilly courses, longer races versus shorter ones, and about how they feel they might fare when faced with a variety of adverse weather conditions. As coaches, we likely have a feel for how they might perform relative to their competition when faced with these various challenges. Get them thinking about it too.

Emily Rypina,

Griffin Coots (#15)

CHAPTER SEVENTEEN

Periodization

Countless books have been written about the concept of periodization as it applies to distance runners and the calendar. There's a reason that this topic gets so much press. Though tremendously important, it is commonly ignored and/or misunderstood by young runners and coaches alike. In our chapter that discussed the degree to which distance running is not a seasonal sport, we talked about the need for a young distance runner who aspires to greatness to continue running year-round. Further, we talked about the degree to which what he or she is running in June might vary from what he or she is running in October. It is, in part, this variation and our body's adaptation thereto that allow us to progress and improve as runners from season to season and year to year.

My approach to the calendar does not vary all that greatly from that of many of the country's top coaches, either at the high school or collegiate levels. There are times of year that call for greater volume and times of year that call for greater intensity. August workouts are August workouts and November workouts are November workouts for a reason, and they are, for the most part, not interchangeable.

If you are on the track doing 200-meter repeats in the middle of June and your primary focus is the cross country season that is still three months hence, I might suggest that, while I very much appreciate your work ethic and enthusiasm, your focus for that particular time of year might be a little off target.

I had a student-athlete not long ago who insisted that the summer was the "time to get faster." Though I strongly advised against it, he could be found doing hard workouts on the track within a week or two of the spring track season having ended, several months ahead of the fall cross country season. Not a great idea. While his work ethic, enthusiasm, and desire to get better were commendable, he was doing himself a great disservice by being quite so workout-oriented at that time of year. Borne of a lack of understanding and experience, I've seen other young runners make similar mistakes throughout the years and the end result is almost always in-season disappointment.

For the high school runner, summer is the time to get stronger, to build your foundation, and to build your base in preparation for the upcoming season. You'll have plenty of time for those agonizing workouts in August, September, and October.

Early-season workouts are generally of the longer and relatively slower variety with minimal recoveries. As an example, mile repeats are commonly a viable, though not enjoyable, early-season option. As the season progresses, the workouts gradually become shorter and faster with longer recoveries. A brisk 10 × 200 meter workout would be far more appropriate to late October than it would be to August, just as you likely wouldn't want to be doing mile repeats as an immediate lead up to your conference championship meet.

I had the pleasure of coaching alongside Mike Wilson at Eastern University several years ago. One of the brightest young coaches in the country, Mike has since coached at the University of Michigan and is currently Head Coach at George Fox University in Oregon. In summarizing a runner's progression through any given training cycle, Mike explains it this way. . . . "Capacity, then power. We have to have capacity before we can have power output. No capacity, no power. Threshold and longer reps early in the season equals capacity. If we can handle higher volumes of less intense levels of work, we set the foundation to be able to handle lower volumes of higher intensity levels later on." There's that term "foundation" again.

By continually running grueling, shorter workouts at all times of the year, you are doing yourself a disservice. You are risking injury and burnout and taking away from time that might be better spent building your strength and foundation. It is very difficult to do both simultaneously. Pay attention to the calendar. Build your base over the summer, increase your aerobic capacity, and get stronger. Give yourself something on which to build when you start easing into those workouts in the late summer and early fall.

In emphasizing the importance of increasing one's strength and building a solid foundation as a runner, my student-athletes have heard me use this analogy on many occasions. "Regardless of how aggressively you approach your workouts during the fall, no matter how committed you are at that point, if you have failed to lay a solid base or foundation during the summer, all you are really doing is putting fancy shingles on a poorly built house." Is it a perfect analogy? No, but I think it gets the point across.

Lastly, don't be afraid to take a little bit of downtime after the season. This doesn't necessarily mean an extended period of no running but it surely suggests periodic days off, no workouts, and maybe some extra sleep. Two or three weeks of relative downtime like this can only do you good, both mentally and physically. Just be careful that "relative downtime" doesn't become "absolute downtime" and that two or three easy weeks doesn't become six or seven easy weeks.

Improvement as a runner rarely comes in a linear progression. The seasons don't change in a linear pattern. The stock market doesn't move in a straight line. Neither will your improvement as a distance runner.

CHAPTER EIGHTEEN

Periodization – Part 2

I'd promised not to get into the nitty-gritty of breaking down various workouts as part of this 1st edition of *Discovering High School Cross Country*. The templates that follow, however, will give you a brief overview and introduction as to how I view the season and try to break it down for my student-athletes. Just as I encourage my runners to "have a plan" going into any particular race, so too do we as coaches, and as a coach-and-runner team, need to "have a plan" as we approach each season and even each week. I always keep electronic as well as printed copies of these personalized templates for review in the future.

Ada Thomsen
Track 2021

Week Beginning	28-Dec	4-Jan	11-Jan	18-Jan	25-Jan	1-Feb	8-Feb	15-Feb	22-Feb	1-Mar	8-Mar	15-Mar	22-Mar	29-Mar	5-Apr	12-Apr	19-Apr	26-Apr	3-May
Mesocycle	1						2 (Pre-Competitive)						Competitive						

Mesocycle Theme

Conditioning / Preparation:
Focus on building / rebuilding for the spring season. Extended Aerobic development and Lactate Threshold development.
Maintain the length of our long runs while assuring enough rest and recovery to minimize risk of injury. One six mile run weekly.
Tempo runs gradually become longer and more aggressive. Workouts are generally more strength-oriented. Longer intervals / lesser recovery.
Weekly mileage to average 28-30, alternating weeks of 1 and 2 days off.

Pre-Competitive:
Begin emphasizing VO2 Max development and Anaerobic endurance.
efficiency and capacity.
Continue to focus on Aerobic capacity, enhancement, and the long-term
Aerobic changes that we began during the 1st Mesocycle.
Workouts gradually become shorter and faster w/ longer recoveries.
We introduce aggressive striders after most long runs.

Competitive:
Emphasize all adaptations needed to perform at full race capacity.
Optimal development of the Anaerobic system
relative to the needs of racing. Maintain proper volume
and intensity relationships, peaking for end-of-season competitions
As part of a proper taper, volume may decrease by as much as 30%
but intensity does not.
Workouts are fast / short with extended recoveries.
(i.e. 8 x 150-200 w/4 min recovery)

Microcycle	1	2	3	4	5	6	7	8	9	10	11	12	13	14	15	16	17	18	19

Our 7-day Microcycles will vary and evolve as we move from one Mesocycle to the next.
Mesocycle 1 will include one weekly Tempo run, one weekly In/out-type of workout,
one weekly long run of 6 miles and either 2 or 3 easy run days of ~5 miles,
depending upon the week.
During Microcycle 4 and 5 we will begin including some shorter and faster efforts.
Some longer, aggressive striders should be included following most longer runs.

Competition / Non Focus
Competition / Focus

Competition letters by week: A, B, C,D, E, F, G (Microcycles 6–11); H,I, J, K, L (Microcycles 12–16); M (Microcycle 18)

Evaluation

	VO2 Max	6.12
	1650	
	400	
	Pushups	
	Situps	
	Planks	

VO2 MAX
1650
400
Pushups
Situps
Planks

Competition Key:

A Preseason Meet at PRHS (2/11)
B Ida Baker Indoor / Outdoor at Ida Baker HS (2/20)
C Bear Invitational at PRHS (2/24)
D Jim Smith Invitational at GGHS (2/27)
E GG Dual Meet (3/3)
F Eagle Invitational at NHS (3/6)
G GG Dual Meet (3/10)
H CCAC Fresh / Soph @ Lely (3/23)
I Terpon Invitational (3/26)
J Wally Keller Invitational @ Charlotte HS (4/1)
K CCAC Championships at NHS (4/9-4/10)
L District Meet - BCHS / NHS (4/16-4/17)
M Regional Meet at Charlotte HS (5/1)

Name: Addie   Event: Cross Country 3K   PR / Year: 12:01 / 2020   Goal: Sub 12:00

Age: 14   Macrocycle: Fall / XC 2021   Mesocycle #: 1   Microcycle #: 7

Day	Date	Training Session	Notes
Mon	9/20	Tempo Run, 30 min. run w/ middle 20 at tempo pace, HR ~ 185, approximated pace is about halfway between that of a normal distance run and the pace that you might anticipate being able to run for 3K	Lactate Tolerance/Threshold
Tues	9/21	Easy distance day, ~ 30-35 mins.	Aerobic Capacity
Weds	9/22	10 x 300 Meters on the track – no spikes w/ 3 min. recovery	Anaerobic Glycolytic / Glyco Power
Thurs	9/23	Easy distance day, ~ 30-35 mins.	Aerobic Capacity
Fri	9/24	Pre-Meet Day, Easy 25-30 min run followed by several aggressive striders on the track	
Sat	9/25	Meet @ GG Golf Course	
Sun	9/26	Off	

Objectives

Monday is important but isn't a killer workout. Were we to go really hard on Monday, it would leave us with 4 max effort days over an 8 day period. That's too much. It's too early to start cutting down to anything shorter than 300s. That will come during the week of October 11th. Consistency is enormously important. Easy days aren't just "filler".

Weight Room

N/A

Warm Up

Beginning with warmup jog of ~ 0.5 mile. Dynamic stretches to include Mock A/B, high knees, quick feet, leg swings, and hurdle mobility. Striders of 80-100 meters at 75 – 80% effort prior to any workouts or competitions. Less concerned about extended warmups on easier days.

Cool Down

Easy jog of ~ 800 meters, light stretching, more passive than dynamic. No need for cooldown on longer, easier days.

Name: Rilee Morrison   Event: 1600   PR / Year: N/A   Goal:

Age: 14 / Freshman   Macrocycle: Spring 2021   Mesocycle #: 1   Microcycle #: 1

Day	Date	Training Session	Notes
Mon	12/28	Tempo run: 40 mins. w/ middle 20 mins. at Tempo pace, HR ~ 175-180 No need to go any faster. HR averaged 185—190 throughout Tempo.	Aerobic capacity / Lactate Threshold
Tues	12/29	Easy 5 miles averaged 8:44 pace, HR ~ 170	Aerobic Capacity / Recovery
Weds	12/30	8 x 60 secs. On/off w/ 10 min jog on either end, 35 mins. total running time HR peaked at ~ 198 during 8 harder portions	First harder effort in 4 weeks. P of V vs. Mon.
Thurs	12/31	Easy 5 miles 5.1 @ 8:07 pace Avg. HR 168	Comfortable? Recovery? Easy off if necessary.
Fri	1/1	VO2 Max test @ North Collier (1600 meter max effort / HR / Weight) 6:02.6 (1:22.8, 2:57.8, 4:32.4, 6:02.6) Max HR 202 Weight 102	Low volume day but max effort.
Sat	1/2	6 Miles @ 9:10 pace	
Sun	1/3	Off	

Objectives

Time to get focused on building / rebuilding for the spring season. Focus during 1st Mesocycle will be on Extended Aerobic development and Extended Lactate Threshold development. Will be looking to maintain length of long runs while working to minimize any risk of injury. Rest day on Saturday. Refresher conversations related to terminologies and concepts: Lactate Threshold, VO2 Max., Principle of Variation, etc.. Goals for spring season?

Weight Room

Warm Up

Beginning with warmup jog of ~ 0.5 mile. Dynamic stretches to include Mock A/B, high knees, quick feet, leg swings, and hurdle mobility. Striders of 80-100 meters at 75 – 80% effort prior to any workouts or competitions. Less concerned about extended warmups on easier days.

Cool Down

Easy jog of up to 1600 meters, light stretching, more passive than dynamic. No need for cooldown on longer, easier days.

CHAPTER NINETEEN

The 3rd, 4th, and 5th runners / Depth Matters!

If put on a graph, cross country meet results would almost always present themselves in a classic "bell curve." The first few runners are commonly spread out by relatively wide margins. The same is true of the last few runners. This is true of races in which there are a few dozen runners as well as races in which there are several hundred. Boys or girls, 5K or 10K, it doesn't matter. It's in the middle of the pack where we find runners finishing fast and furious, another runner crossing the finish line every couple of seconds. This is most commonly where a good team's third, fourth, and fifth runners are finishing. Accordingly, one could argue that this is where many meets are won and lost from a team perspective.

Not to be misconstrued, most championship teams need to have those elite runners, those who finish among the top few places in any given race. However, let's consider the importance of the third, fourth, and fifth runner from this perspective. . . . Fiona Smith from College of St. Benedict won the recently concluded NCAA Division III Women's National Cross-Country Championship meet by an incredible one minute and three seconds. That's ridiculous! She could have run a full minute slower and still won the race. Similarly, she could have run ten, twenty, or thirty seconds faster and won by an even more impressive margin. Either way, whether she ran 30 seconds faster or 30 seconds slower, her team's score for the meet would not have changed. First place is first place. Either way, your team accrues one point towards its total score. Remember, your top five runners score. Their finish places are added together and the low score wins.

Now consider Leah White, a freshman from Bates College who finished 149th in the same race in a very solid 22:50. There were 292 finishers in the race. Accordingly, 149th place was right in the middle of the pack, right in the middle of that "bell curve." Had Leah somehow managed to run 30 seconds faster on that particular day, she would have jumped from 149th all the way up to 82nd place, an incredible jump of 67 places. As a result, Bates would have finished 25th as a team rather than 29th. Had Leah run 30 seconds slower, she would have fallen all the way back to 230th place, adding an enormous 81 points to Bates' team score. A thirty-second variation either way would have meant essentially nothing to Ms. Smith and her College of St. Benedict team. That same 30-second variation, however, if applied to Ms. White and her team from Bates, could have had significant ramifications

I'd intended to include complete results from this particular meet as part of this writing only to realize that it would have taken the better part of six or seven pages to do so. Those results are readily available at https://www.leonetiming.com/2023/XC/NCAAD3Women.htm.

As you review the results of various cross country meets, pay particular attention to where any given team's third, fourth, and fifth runners are finishing. In most cases, you'll likely be amazed at the degree to which they are the ones affecting that meet's outcome and influencing their team's score the most. I can't count how many times I have heard "Coach, I don't really matter that much, I'm only our number five runner" or something along those lines. Not true. The numbers bear out that your 3rd, 4th, and 5th runners can be enormously important.

As another example of just how important team depth can be . . . several years ago I'd had the opportunity to return to my high school alma mater to watch their league championship meet. They had a couple of very talented runners on their boys' team that fall. Their league is small, only six schools, meaning that there would be only 42 boys competing in the varsity race that afternoon, 7 varsity athletes per school, as is the norm. As was probably expected, their top two runners finished in 1st and 2nd. Their 3rd runner on that particular day finished in 4th place overall. Seemingly they were well on their way to a lopsided team championship. Over the next several minutes, however, runner after runner crossed the finish line, none of whom were wearing the red and white of my former high school. Following the exceptional performances of their top three runners, their next runner finished in 35th place. That was followed by a 39th place finish, then 40th, and 42nd. Not only did they fail to win the meet, they finished in third place, two points behind the league champions and one point out of 2nd place as a team. That's almost impossible. The math hardly makes sense. I might not have believed it myself if I hadn't seen it. They didn't need their 4th or 5th runners to be superstars on that particular day. Had one of them even managed to finish in 32nd or 33rd place, they would have been team champions.

While this is an extreme example, stories like these are not uncommon. The moral here is this… Even if you are "only" the 4th or 5th runner on your team, you can still be of enormous importance. For that matter, the same thing applies if you are 6th or 7th runner on your team and are aspiring to move up. Don't underestimate your ability to affect the final outcome of any given meet.

Landon Turner and Mia Metcalf: Never underestimate what you might be able to contribute to your team. First runner? Seventh runner? It doesn't matter.

CHAPTER TWENTY

Team Captains

Different coaches handle the team captain question in different ways. Some choose not to have team captains at all. That may well be the right answer for some. No two sets of circumstances are quite the same.

As a young runner myself, I grew up in an environment in which we usually had team captains and I prefer to follow that structure now as a coach. Most commonly, I prefer to leave the captain-selection process up to the kids, usually in the form of anonymous ballots and a nominating process if necessary. The number of captains on any given team might vary based upon the size of the team and the personalities involved. The student-athletes seemingly know what they are looking for when it comes to selecting their leaders. To date, I cannot recall a single instance in which the kids did not pick the appropriate captain(s).

Before allowing the student-athletes to begin the captain-selection process, I usually stress two things . . .

1. Being captain means more than merely getting your picture in the yearbook. It means more than simply being the one to lead warmups at practice every afternoon. It brings with it certain

leadership responsibilities and expectations. It assumes confidentiality when there are issues within the team. A captain doesn't tell the freshmen to take down the tent and pack it on the bus after a meet; a captain helps take care of it himself. A captain is essentially an extension of me as coach.

2. Captains are most commonly seniors and among the best runners on a given team but it doesn't necessarily have to be that way. Presumably, and I'm making some big assumptions here, seniors have usually been around for a while. They have learned about work ethic and leadership. They have honed their communications skills. They've won and they've lost. They've made mistakes and learned from those mistakes. They have earned the respect of their teammates and coaches. That's why they oftentimes make the best captains. If all of those things can be said about a particular sophomore or junior, so be it. He or she should likely be considered as a possible captain. I have seen plenty of those over the years. I am of the opinion that a captain should never be selected merely based upon their level of seniority nor natural talent as a runner.

On one occasion, I went so far as to appoint a freshman as captain. I spoke to her about it beforehand and explained to her that she and I would likely both receive some negative pushback as a result, but I felt that it was appropriate for several reasons: Her maturity was already on par with that of many of the juniors and seniors. Her work ethic was well above average. Her upside potential as a runner was considerable and she seemed to have already garnered the respect of most of the upperclassmen. Also part of the equation was the fact that our team stunk and I knew that by the time we were back to a point of relevance, she would likely be a junior or senior and she and the team would have had the opportunity to grow together. I took a chance and it turned out exactly as I had hoped it would.

More recently, I had a young lady named Ada serve as cross country co-captain during both her junior and senior seasons in high school. Ada wasn't commonly among our top three or four runners but she brought other attributes to the table, qualities and characteristics that made appointing her one of our captains an easy decision. Without necessarily intending to be, she was an obvious leader. "As goes Ada, so goes the team." I knew it and her teammates knew it.

Ada Thomsen: Though not our top runner, her leadership skills and the degree to which the other girls looked up to her and followed her lead made Ada an obvious choice for captain.

CHAPTER TWENTY-ONE

Issues of Form and Function

This is one of those topics on which I will largely defer to the exercise physiologists and kinesiologists among us. Concerns related to proper running form can be exceedingly complicated. Issues of form and function can oftentimes lead to injuries and a lack of running efficiency. In other instances, they are little more than quirky habits that are best left alone.

Here again, I refer to Mike Wilson, the Head Coach at George Fox University. His ability to identify and diagnose various issues related to one's running form is among the best I've ever seen. I have to admit to being a bit envious of his abilities along those lines.

We have all been at meets where we've heard coaches and parents alike yelling to their runners "lift your knees," "drop your arms," or something similar. They are well intentioned for sure and, in all likelihood, they have identified legitimate issues that probably need to be addressed.

My concern is this, however. To what degree are those encouraging words of "lift your knees" and "drop your arms" addressing the root cause of the issue if, in fact, there is an issue at all? Lower knee lift and higher arm carriage are most commonly symptoms of an underlying issue rather than being issues in and of themselves. Are there muscular imbalances involved? Might stretching and strengthening certain muscle groups help to alleviate the problem?

If you were to come to me with a headache every day and I were simply to give you an Advil, I am really only treating your symptoms and am doing nothing to find out why you are getting these constant headaches. Though the analogy is not perfect, am I not really only doing the same thing when I constantly remind you to "lift your knees" and "drop your arms"?

I've found it helps immensely to use video in identifying and diagnosing form-related issues. It's remarkable how much the human eye can miss in real time.

Some athletic trainers are highly proficient at addressing issues of form. Others, not so much. When in doubt, don't hesitate to seek out a professional. They can oftentimes be costly but the vast majority of them really know what they are doing and can be very helpful.

Knee lift, arm carriage angles, point of impact, foot strike.
It's all part of the form-and-function equation.

CHAPTER TWENTY-TWO

Peaking and Tapering

In an ideal world, we are running at our very best during those last three to four weeks of the season when it really matters the most: conference championships, districts, regionals, and nationals. That's when we want to be at our "peak." On many occasions I've heard coaches and runners talk about trying to peak at multiple times during a single season. That is exceedingly difficult. Trying to peak once is difficult enough. Unless you are an athlete of national or even international stature, the need to peak more than once during any given season likely doesn't even exist. Thankfully.

It is probably unrealistic to expect to remain at your peak for more than three to four weeks. I've seen it done but it is rare.

A well-executed taper includes a decrease in total running volume but not necessarily a decrease in intensity. Trial and error and significant study have taught me that the ideal mileage decrease is probably somewhere in the 30% range over those last ten to fourteen days prior to your first postseason meet. A runner who has been running 50 miles per week consistently throughout the seasons may now drop it down to about 35. As we talked about earlier, our workouts have continued to, on average, become shorter and faster with longer recoveries during the course of the season. Our days of mile repeats are now long behind us and we have gradually transitioned down to 200s, 300s, and 400s. The recoveries have grown longer in the interest of allowing the body energy system most responsible for pure speed to more fully replenish itself in between repetitions. Failure to do so forces the body to begin drawing more energy from the other energy systems within our body, those which are secondary to absolute speed.

Gibson Ardoline

Taylor Morrison

CHAPTER TWENTY-THREE

Injuries

Running-related injuries are brutal. There is no such thing as good time for an injury but they always seem to come around at the absolute worst possible times. Some are relatively minor and may ease within a couple of days. Others, not so much. In this book's introduction I suggested that "if there is an injury to be had, I probably had it." I underwent six reconstructive surgical procedures during my own running career in the interest of being able to continue pursuing the sport that I loved. "Rehab" was a word that I became all too familiar with.

As a coach, shin splints are by the far the most common injury that I hear about during any given season. Accordingly, let's talk briefly about shin-related issues. We can save a more detailed conversation about running-related injuries for a later time.

In our day-to-day lives we really ask very little of the muscles in the anterior portion of our lower legs. They are essentially just along for the ride most of the time. Suddenly, we decide to go out for cross country and those muscles that we can collectively refer to as being our "shin muscles" (primarily the tibialis anterior) don't like it. They're not used to having to work so hard, and soreness and inflammation are oftentimes quick to develop.

At their onset, shin splits may be little more than a dull ache that comes and goes. At their worst, shin splints can be excruciating, making running virtually impossible. The trick with shin splints is to try to avoid getting them in the first place. Once you've gotten them, they can be hard to get rid of. If you've not been particularly active of late and you know that the cross country season is quickly approaching, you might consider doing some exercises specifically designed to strengthen those very muscles. I tend to hear many more complaints about shin splints early in the season than I do later.

You can use a simple exercise band to perform a variety of stretching and strengthening exercises, pitting one foot against the other to help build those shin muscles. Do two or three sets of twelve or more repetitions each at least once per day. You'll very quickly begin to "feel the burn." That tells you that you're doing it right. If formal exercise bands are not available, you can do the exact same thing by taking an old bicycle inner tube and making one of your own.

Be proactive in addressing those shin issues. You don't want to wait until those muscles are sore and inflamed to begin your strengthening exercises. That will only exacerbate the problem.

If you've already reached the point of soreness, several days of rest and ice will usually help ease the inflammation to the point that you can begin a strengthening routine like the one I've outlined. Give that inflammation some time to calm down. Don't try to be a hero by doing your shin-blasting exercises while they are still tender.

Running on softer surfaces and assuring that your shoes are in good condition can help alleviate some of the pain but, as I mentioned earlier in my chapter on issues related to biomechanical issues, ice and ibuprofen are only treating the symptoms of your injury; they are not addressing the root cause.

A simple resistance band can be made out of an old bike tire inner tube, as shown. Exercises like these can go a long way towards preventing shin splint issues. While seated, place the right foot on top of the left with the band around the forefoot. The bottom foot acts as resistance and the right heel remains in contact with the top of the left foot. Pull your right forefoot upwards, then relax and repeat. Do a set of 15 and then switch feet. Similarly, to work the lateral sides of both shins, put one heel against the other and pull outwards with both forefeet simultaneously.

CHAPTER TWENTY-FOUR

What's Next?

On several occasions over the course of having written this book, I've found myself so motivated and so fired up about running that I've needed to shut down my laptop and go out for a run myself. The degree to which this book has motivated me, however, is of very little significance. My hope is that is has motivated you!

I routinely tell my younger runners, "I can't promise to make you the fastest runner in the league, in the district, or in the region but, if you are willing to work at it, I can help to make you one of the smartest." In this sport, "smarts" go a long, long way. I've seen that proven to be true time and time and time again. I hope that this book has helped you in that process.

I've already received a lot of early feedback asking for more details and more specifics on a variety of the topics that we've talked about over these past many pages. It's coming. A second edition is already in the works.

As part of that 2nd edition, we will get into more specifics related to the microcycle, macrocycle, and mesocycle training concept. We'll talk in more detail about the body's energy systems. We will introduce some significantly more scientific concepts along the lines of VO2 Max.

We will expand upon our conversations about injuries and proper warmups and cooldowns. We will talk about gender-specific issues related to high school–age distance runners and we will talk about appropriate footwear choices and options. In the meantime, as I did at one of our recent end-of-season awards banquets, I want to leave you with this. . . .

Try to avoid the natural tendency to say "could have." "I could have" done this. "I could have" done that. We all know someone who is constantly talking about all of the things that he or she "could have" done. Have you ever noticed, however, that those who are constantly talking about all of the things that they "could have" done are usually the ones *least* likely to have been able to do all of those things in the first place? "I 'could have' gone to the prom with Jennifer if I'd asked her." "I 'could have' passed biology if I'd studied a little more."

In this context, think of this concept specifically as it applies to your running career. "I 'could have' made varsity if I had run more over the summer." "I 'could have' broken my PR at districts if I'd run a little smarter." Try to avoid putting yourself in a position where "could have" is even a viable choice of words.

Are there variables such as injuries and illness that might come along from time to time that leave us all pondering and postulating about what might have been? Absolutely. Let others talk about what you might have been able to do if they choose to do so. There's nothing wrong with that.

As I said at the outset, you've stumbled onto something good. Prepare yourself for the inevitable ups and down of our great sport. Be willing to embrace those challenging times, knowing that they only serve to make those good times that much better.